Dream BIG

American Idol SUPERSTARS

Kris Allen

David Archuleta

Kelly Clarkson

David Cook

Chris Daughtry

Jennifer Hudson

Adam Lambert

Kellie Pickler

Jordin Sparks

Carrie Underwood

Elliott Yamin

American Idol Profiles Index:
Top Finalists from Seasons 1 to 7
(82 Contestants)

Insights Into American Idol

Chris Daughtry

Hal Marcovitz

Mason Crest Publishers

Produced by 21st Century Publishing and Communications, Inc.

MASON CREST PUBLISHERS INC.
370 Reed Road
Broomall, Pennsylvania 19008
(866) MCP-BOOK (toll free)
www.masoncrest.com

Printed in the United States of America.

First Printing

9 8 7 6 5 4 3 2 1

Library of Congress Cataloging-in-Publication Data

Marcovitz, Hal.
  Chris Daughtry / Hal Marcovitz.
     p. cm. — (Dream big: American Idol superstars)
  Includes bibliographical references and index.
  ISBN 978-1-4222-1508-1 (hardback : alk. paper)
  ISBN 978-1-4222-1595-1 (pbk. : alk. paper)
   1. Daughtry, Chris, 1979–   —Juvenile literature. 2. Rock musicians—United
States—Biography—Juvenile literature. I. Title.
ML3930.D325M37 2010
782.42166092—dc22
  [B]   2009021193

Publisher's notes:
All quotations in this book come from original sources, and contain the spelling and grammatical inconsistencies of the original text.

The Web sites mentioned in this book were active at the time of publication. The publisher is not responsible for Web sites that have changed their addresses or discontinued operation since the date of publication. The publisher will review and update the Web site addresses each time the book is reprinted.

American Idol ® is a registered trademark of 19 TV Ltd. and FremantleMedia North America, Inc.

CONTENTS

American Idol TIMELINE ★

October 5, 2001

Pop Idol, a TV reality show created by Simon Fuller, debuts in the United Kingdom and becomes a smash hit.

Fall 2001

Based on the success of *Pop Idol*, and after initially rejecting the concept, FOX Network agrees to buy *American Idol*, a national talent competition and TV reality show.

Spring 2002

Auditions for *American Idol* Season 1 are held in New York City, Los Angeles, Chicago, Dallas, Miami, Atlanta, and Seattle.

January 21, 2003

American Idol Season 2 premieres without Brian Dunkleman, leaving Ryan Seacrest as the sole host.

May 21, 2003

- *American Idol* Season 2 finale airs.
- Ruben Studdard narrowly wins and Clay Aiken is the runner-up.
- Runner-up Clay Aiken goes on to become extremely successful both critically and commercially.

January 19, 2004

American Idol Season 3 premieres.

2001   2002   2003   2004

June 11, 2002

American Idol Season 1 premieres on FOX Network, with Simon Cowell, Paula Abdul, and Randy Jackson as the judges, and Ryan Seacrest and Brian Dunkleman as the co-hosts.

September 4, 2002

- *American Idol* Season 1 finale airs.
- Kelly Clarkson wins and Justin Guarini is the runner-up.
- Kelly Clarkson goes on to become the most successful Idol winner and a superstar in the music industry.

Fall 2002

Auditions for *American Idol* Season 2 are held in New York City, Los Angeles, Miami, Detroit, Nashville, and Austin.

January 27, 2004

William Hung's audition is aired and his humble response to Simon Cowell's scathing criticism make William the most famous American Idol non-qualifier and earn him record deals and a cult-like following.

April 21, 2004

Jennifer Hudson is voted off the show in 7th place, and goes on to win the role of Effie in *Dreamgirls*, for which she wins an Academy Award, a Golden Globe Award, and a Grammy Award.

May 26, 2004

- *American Idol* Season 3 finale airs with 65 million viewers casting their votes.
- Fantasia Barrino is crowned the winner and Diana DeGarmo is the runner-up.
- Fantasia soon becomes the first artist in the history of Billboard to debut at number one with her first single.

May 10, 2006

Chris Daughtry is voted off the show in 4th place, and soon after forms the band, Daughtry, and releases its debut album, which becomes number one on the charts, wins many awards, and finds huge commercial success.

April 26, 2006

Kellie Pickler is voted off the show in 6th place, and soon releases her debut album, which rockets to number one on the Billboard Top Country Album chart.

January 17, 2006

American Idol Season 5 premieres and for the first time airs in high definition.

May 24, 2006

- *American Idol* Season 5 finale airs.
- Taylor Hicks is the winner and Katharine McPhee the runner-up.
- Elliot Yamin, the second runner-up, goes on to release his debut album, which goes gold.

January 16, 2007

American Idol Season 6 premieres.

April 2007

The *American Idol* Songwriting Contest is announced.

January 15, 2008

American Idol Season 7 airs with a four-hour two-day premiere.

April 9, 2008

Idol Gives Back returns for its second year.

May 21, 2008

- *American Idol* Season 7 finale airs.
- David Cook wins with 54.6 million votes and David Archuleta is the runner-up with 42.9 million votes.
- Both Davids go on to tremendous post-Idol success with successful albums and singles.

2005 2006 2007 2008 2009

May 25, 2005

- *American Idol* Season 4 finale airs.
- Carrie Underwood wins and Bo Bice is the runner-up.
- Carrie goes on to become one of the most successful Idol winners, selling millions of albums and winning scores of major awards.

January 18, 2005

- *American Idol* Season 4 premieres.
- Some rules change:
  - The age limit is raised from 24 to 28.
  - The semi-final competition is separated by gender up until the 12 finalists.

April 24–25, 2007

American Idol Gives Back, a charitable campaign to raise money for underprivileged children worldwide, airs, and raises more than $70 million.

May 23, 2007

- *American Idol* Season 6 finale airs.
- Jordin Sparks wins with 74 million votes and Blake Lewis is the runner-up.
- Jordin goes on to join Kelly Clarkson and Carrie Underwood in the ranks of highly successful post-Idol recording artists.

January 13, 2009

American Idol Season 8 premieres adding Kara DioGuardi as a fourth judge.

February 14, 2009

The American Idol Experience, a theme park attraction, officially opens at Disney's Hollywood Studio in Florida.

May 20, 2009

- *American Idol* Season 8 finale airs.
- Kris Allen unexpectedly wins and Adam Lambert is the runner-up.
- Almost 100 million people voted in the season 8 finale.

Chris Daughtry's powerful style was new to national audiences when he appeared in *American Idol,* but he quickly gained many die-hard fans. Less than two years after the competition, his first album became the fastest selling rock CD in history and was nominated for four Grammy awards.

1

New to the Game

Chris Daughtry's world moved very quickly after the singer from North Carolina was voted off *American Idol* in May 2006. He signed a record contract and cut an enormously successful album. Then, not quite two years since leaving *Idol,* Chris found himself surrounded by the top names in music as he attended the 2008 Grammy Awards in Los Angeles.

He had been nominated for four Grammy Awards for his debut album, titled *Daughtry*. Just a few weeks after its release, the album had been declared **platinum**, meaning it sold more than a million copies. In fact, *Daughtry* proved so successful that it became the fastest selling debut **rock** album in history and would eventually go on to sell more than four million copies. In an interview shortly before the Grammy Awards ceremony, Chris said he owed the success of *Daughtry* to the fans who remained dedicated to his music after he left *American Idol*. He said,

> **❝The only thing I can really attribute it to is the fan base. They're certainly very diehard and loyal to us, and they've continued to buy our record. They've continued to come to our shows. It doesn't matter how good you are as a band or how good your music may be, if the fans aren't supporting it and buying your music, it's hard to make it. So they're the ones that are making it for us.❞**

Hard Rocker

There is no question that during the nearly five months he was a part of *American Idol*, Chris emerged as a real fan favorite. Unlike most other *Idol* performers, who tend to sing **pop** music, Chris regards himself as a hard rocker. The fans as well as *Idol*'s tough panel of judges embraced his electrifying music, supporting him through the early rounds and then voting him into the top tier of competitors. But Chris's luck finally ran out on May 10, 2006, the evening after he covered two Elvis Presley hits. Still, he had made it into the competition's top four.

Winners of *American Idol* are guaranteed million-dollar recording contracts as well as a tremendous amount of national exposure and hype. Others who have come close to winning have also carved out successful recording careers. And so when Chris left *American Idol*, he joined a growing group of ex-*Idol* competitors who have become just as successful in their post-*Idol* careers as the performers who won the competitions. In addition to Chris, that group includes such former *Idol* favorites as Jennifer

Chris thinks of himself as a hard rocker, in contrast to other *Idol* contestants who were mainly pop singers. His electrifying style made him stand out in the early rounds. Loyal fans and the judges agreed he had something special and voted him into the group of top four finalists.

Hudson and Elliott Yamin. Said Mitch Allan, a singer, guitarist, and co-writer of one of the tracks on *Daughtry*,

> **❝[Losing] was the best thing that could have happened to him. Chris got booted off because America knew he was a rock guy on a pop show. It reaffirmed his rock status. He's not a pop tart . . . He would have been a rock star with or without *American Idol*.❞**

WHEN LOSING IS AS GOOD AS WINNING

Elliott Yamin has come close to matching Chris's record as the most successful *Idol* contestant not to win the competition. During the show's fifth season, he lasted just one week longer than Chris. Soon after leaving the show, he cut an album, *Elliott Yamin*, which debuted in the top position on *Billboard* magazine's Top Independent Albums chart as well as in third place on the *Billboard* 200.

Jennifer Hudson has also emerged as one of the top stars in America. Jennifer competed in the show's third season and although she made it into the top 10, she was voted off well before the finals. Soon after leaving the show, Jennifer won a part in the film *Dreamgirls* and went on to win an Academy Award for Best Supporting Actress and record a hit album, titled *Jennifer Hudson*.

Dazzled by Bright Lights

In late 2007, the National Academy of Recording Arts & Sciences, which sponsors the Grammy Awards, announced the nominations for 2008. Chris was nominated for four of the awards, including Best Rock Album for *Daughtry*, Best Performance by a Pop or Musical Group for the single "Home," Best Performance by a Rock or Musical Group for the single "It's Not Over," and Best Rock Song for "It's Not Over."

On February 8, 2008, Chris attended the awards ceremony. Dressed in black leather pants, vest, and jacket, Chris was accompanied up the red carpet by his wife, Deanna Robertson. He admitted to being dazzled by the bright lights and the excitement of attending the Grammys as a nominee. Not quite two years before, Chris had been working in the service department of a car dealership; now he found himself surrounded by the likes of Fergie, Janet Jackson, and Whitney Houston.

For Chris, unfortunately, it would not prove to be a night of triumph. He did not win in any of the categories in which he was nominated. After the show, Chris said he held no hard feelings and is looking forward to getting on with his career. Pleased to have been nominated in the first place, he said,

Chris, his wife Deanna Robertson, and his fellow band members were amazed by the scene at the 2008 Grammy Awards. Not only had Chris been nominated for four Grammys, but he was also on the same red carpet with glittering superstars of the music industry whom he had always admired.

"Last year, it was like [being] a freshman in high school who wants to hang out with the seniors. This year, we're still new to the game, but we feel like we're slowly but surely graduating to our senior year."

Chris grew up in the backwoods of North Carolina and Virginia and helped his parents on their farm. His dream of becoming a hard rocker started in high school when he learned to play the guitar. Chris performed in local bands and idolized rock groups like Pearl Jam and Live.

Backwoods Beginning

The Blue Gator Bar in Burlington, North Carolina, is dark, tiny, and off the main road. In other words, it's the type of place where young rockers go to find an audience and a small paycheck. Back in 2005, no young rocker was working harder for a smaller paycheck than Chris Daughtry.

In fact, at the end of the night, Chris and the three other members of his band, Absent Element, split the money the bar owner paid them to entertain the small crowds. The average paycheck for each band member? About $25.

Each week, Chris and the other band members practiced and played hard, but each week success seemed to elude them. Recalled Chris,

❝It was a real discouraging time. I always felt like, 'Next year, we'll have a record deal.' But years went by and nothing happened. It was horrible.❞

Picking Potatoes

Chris was born on December 26, 1979, in the small town of Roanoke Rapids in North Carolina, just a few miles south of the Virginia border. He was raised first in Lasker, another small North Carolina town. As a teenager, his family moved to Palmyra, just across the Virginia border. For a time, the Daughtry family owned a small farm where Chris picked potatoes and corn. For Chris, it was definitely a backwoods boyhood.

As Chris grew older, he worked alongside his father at a sawmill and then found a job at a McDonald's. As a boy, he was fascinated by the **martial arts** and saw himself as an action movie star in the mold of Jean-Claude Van Damme. But he also

INFLUENCED BY BON JOVI

Chris has long admired the work of the rock band Bon Jovi. During his first national TV performance on *Idol*, Chris sang the Bon Jovi hit "Wanted Dead or Alive." After leaving *Idol*, Chris toured with Bon Jovi, opening the band's concerts and at times sharing the stage with the band.

Since Bon Jovi formed in 1984, it has sold more than 100 million albums. The band is led by singer and guitarist Jon Bon Jovi, who was born John Bongiovi Jr. in 1962. Bon Jovi grew up in Sayreville, New Jersey, and graduated from Sayreville High School in 1980. The song "Wanted Dead or Alive" is from the band's 1987 album, *Slippery When Wet*, which was the third Bon Jovi album. "Wanted Dead or Alive" is a tribute to the outlaws of the Old West. Says Chris,

❝It's an honor to be in a class of people you couldn't get away from on the radio growing up. Those guys are still in the game and it's an encouragement to us, in that maybe we can be that act people are listening to 20 years from now.❞

developed a talent for art and for a time hoped to be a comic book artist.

At the age of 16, Chris learned how to play the guitar, discovered rock 'n' roll, and polished his talent as a singer. At Fluvanna High School in Palmyra he was cast in such school musicals as *The Wiz* and *Peter Pan* while, after school, he performed in makeshift rock bands with his friends. Along the way he earned a few extra dollars singing **country and western** songs at his grandfather's bar, but his heart was truly devoted to hard rock. As a young performer, he admired such bands as Bon Jovi,

One of Chris's early influences was the band Bon Jovi, which has sold more than 100 million albums. Chris sang a Bon Jovi hit on *American Idol,* and after the *Idol* season, he was overjoyed to tour with the band he had once admired from his small-town home.

Bush, Live, Pearl Jam, Alice in Chains, Soundgarden, Stone Temple Pilots, Journey, and Fuel. Recalls Chris,

> **"It seemed like such an awesome world to be a part of, such a cool job. I didn't have a full understanding of music yet. I just wanted to be consumed by it. I wanted to emulate Live."**

Chris and his wife Deanna Robertson live with their children in North Carolina. Only a few years ago, he worked a day job to support the family. He kept his dream of being a rock star by playing with his local band, but never got the big break he hoped for—until *American Idol*.

Missing the Cut

Graduating from high school in 1998, Chris found jobs at a home improvement center, an appliance rental company and, finally, landed behind the service counter at an auto dealership in nearby Greensboro, North Carolina. He admits now that he wasn't a very good employee—often daydreaming about music and writing songs in his head. "I got on my boss's nerves a lot," he says.

At the age of 20, he married Deanna Robertson, who already had two children from a prior marriage. Chris and Deanna moved into a home in McLeansville in suburban Greensboro, and have since added to their family with two of their own children.

After moving to McLeansville, Chris continued performing nights and weekends but his career never seemed to get off the ground. With some friends he started Absent Element, which played local **gigs** and even recorded a CD in 2005. That year, Chris had an audition for a reality show, *Rock Star: INXS*, which sought a new singer for the Australian rock band INXS. He impressed the producers with his audition but, ultimately, did not make the cut for the televised competition. He returned to North Carolina and Absent Element's low-paying gigs and wondered whether he would ever catch a break. He says,

"It was very difficult to get the exposure that I needed to make it where I was from. Having a family and everything, I wasn't exactly financially able to just get in a van and see what happens. So I would just play gigs when I could near [my home], and I would never get the exposure in front of the right people."

Chris hesitated to audition for *American Idol* because so few contestants had been hard rockers. Finally, because his band wasn't doing well, he threw himself into the competition, hoping to get in front of some new people. Chris never guessed how many millions would become his fans.

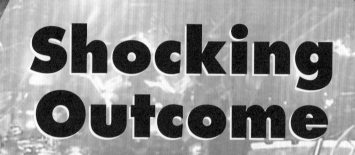

Shocking Outcome

When Chris's wife Deanna suggested he audition for *American Idol*, Chris thought she was joking. Even though the show was now entering its fifth season, and had grown into an enormously successful part of the American entertainment culture, Chris was hardly a fan. Besides, Chris considered himself a hard rocker and everyone knew *Idol* performers were mostly pop singers.

By then, though, it was clear that Chris's musical career had hit a roadblock. Chris and his band, Absent Element, couldn't find anything other than low-paying gigs at local nightclubs in the Greensboro area. A record contract seemed like only a dream. And so, Chris shrugged and decided he had nothing to lose. He said,

> **"I always thought [*Idol*] was a little corny for what I was trying to do. I didn't think it would cater to the rock community. . . . Then I said I might as well try [*Idol*] because it's obviously in front of a lot of people. So it's either going to get my face on TV long enough to get me some more gigs around town, or it's going to take on a life of its own."**

American Idol has been wildly popular since it debuted in 2002. Judges (from left) Randy Jackson, Paula Abdul, and Simon Cowell colorfully critique hopeful performers, and devoted viewers call in to choose competitors for the next round. By the season Chris Daughtry competed, 63 million fans voted for their favorites.

Most Popular Show on TV

From the moment the show premiered on the Fox network in 2002, *American Idol* established itself as one of the most popular programs on TV. Each week, competitors aim toward the eventual prize of a $1 million recording contract along with the national fame and stardom the show virtually guarantees. The show is actually based on its British version, *Pop Idol*, which premiered the year before. Now, versions of *Idol* can be seen in some 35 countries in North America, South America, Europe, and Asia.

The concept is simple: Unknown performers are given opportunities to sing in front of a national audience each week and are assessed on their talents first by a panel of judges and then by audience members at home who vote by phone. To survive the competition, the performers must be approved first by the judges and then by the voters. Each week, the contestant who scores the lowest total of votes is dropped from the competition, although contestants have various opportunities to get back onto the show through so-called "wild card" rounds.

The devotion by millions of fans to the show is overwhelming. By the start of the 2009 season *Forbes* magazine ranked *American Idol* as one of the most successful television shows on the air, earning Fox nearly $30 million a week in TV commercial sales. In the year in which Chris participated, more than 63 million fans cast votes in the finals. Moreover, the show has produced several recording stars, including Kelly Clarkson, Carrie Underwood, and Jennifer Hudson. Says Michael Jung, a Hollywood entertainment executive,

❝It gives you a taste of that next Cinderella story. You could be the next 'American Idol.' It's so organic to the new American dream: It's all about celebrity and fame. But what I really respect about *American Idol* is it's really talent based.❞

The Audition Process

In the weeks preceding the national competition, auditions are held in a number of cities where the panel of judges—Simon Cowell, Randy Jackson, and Paula Abdul—decide who gets to go to Hollywood. Since it is not unusual for some 10,000 people to line up in each city for auditions, the competitors must first audition before *Idol* producers, who decide which contestant gets to sing for a minute or so in front of the judges.

Each year, the series starts out on a humorous note as many of the vocally challenged contestants are given opportunities to sing before the judges. As they warble off-key and out of tune, the camera pans over the faces of Randy, Simon, and Paula, who make little effort to hide their contempt for the no-talent performers. In most cases, it falls to Simon to bluntly tell the singers they should give up their dreams of a recording career. Says Simon,

> **❝I'm actually quite happy when a 17-year-old walks in and sings badly. I tell them they sing badly, and they go, 'Thank you for saving me from a lifetime of pain.' No problem—shake my hand! Enjoy your life.❞**

Talent and Nerve

In early 2006, Chris flew to Denver, Colorado, where he found himself one of about 9,000 contestants preparing to audition. He made it through the preliminary tryouts before the producers and was then invited to sing before Simon, Randy, and Paula. To audition before the judges, Chris chose to sing "The Letter," a somber love ballad by 1970s British rocker Joe Cocker.

After hearing Chris sing a few bars, Randy said, "I liked you. You were in tune, you've got a good voice. It was a little forced, but I like that. It's kind of your style." But Simon, who has a reputation for leveling harsh criticism at young singers, was far less impressed. He said, "I thought you rushed the song.

Chris arrived at the *Idol* audition in Denver to find 9,000 other people in line. He was discouraged when he didn't impress judges Randy and Simon. But when Paula voted yes, Chris raced to share his excitement with Deanna, as he shouted that he would be going to Hollywood.

I'm not sure I saw a lot of charisma. I'm not sure I'm looking at a stand-alone star." And with that, he voted against sending Chris to Hollywood.

The final decision was Paula's, who definitely liked what she heard. "I heard talent and I saw nerve," proclaimed Paula. She voted in favor of the rocker from North Carolina. A few seconds later, Chris burst into the hallway and embraced Deanna, making it clear he had been picked for the national competition.

PAULA ABDUL: CHRIS'S BIGGEST BOOSTER

From the moment Chris auditioned, *American Idol* judge Paula Abdul was his biggest fan. At Chris's audition, after judge Randy Jackson gave Chris the thumbs up but judge Simon Cowell disagreed, Paula cast the deciding vote that sent Chris to Hollywood and ensured his place in the *Idol* competition.

A former Los Angeles Lakers cheerleader, Paula went on to become a much sought after singer, dancer, and choreographer. Her 1988 album, *Forever Your Girl*, made it to the top of the *Billboard* charts.

During the competition, after Chris performed a hard rock version of the Johnny Cash country ballad, "I Walk the Line," Paula shrieked, clapped her hands above her head and said,

> **"You are so true to who you are and you don't ever abandon it. That's what's so amazing about you. You grow and grow each week. You should already be touring and we should be buying tickets."**

When Chris was finally voted off the show, Paula fell into tears.

Idol's Biggest Year

In his first national TV performance on February 22, Chris sang "Dead or Alive" by Bon Jovi. He easily made it through the first round as well as the next two weeks, singing hits by the rock groups Fuel and Seether. But what makes *American Idol* challenging to its competitors is that they have to perform music outside their strongest **genres**. For the first three weeks

At Chris's *Idol* audition, Paula said she immediately saw his talent and nerve shining through. Throughout the competition, Paula applauded Chris's style and growth as an artist and encouraged him as he went on to other rounds. When he was voted off, Paula cried bitter tears.

of the competition, Chris performed only rock songs but by the fourth week, the contestants were instructed to sing hits by **rhythm and blues** legend Stevie Wonder. Chris sang Stevie Wonder's hit "Higher Ground," performing it to a hard rock beat, clearly serving notice that he planned to rely on his strengths.

The judges as well as the audience praised his effort, voting Chris into the competition's top 12. As the weeks moved on, Chris

Chris found fierce competition among other *Idol* top 12 performers. So many hopefuls seemed amazingly gifted that it was impossible to guess who would win. Even the usually grumpy Simon said he was enjoying the wide range of talented contestants like Elliott, Katharine, Chris, Kellie, Bucky, and Taylor.

performed pop songs, love ballads, and even **jazz** standards with that same hard-rocking energy.

By then, the fifth season was shaping up as the most talent-rich season in the history of *American Idol.* As Chris proceeded through the competition, he found himself in the company of some truly astounding performers, including Elliott Yamin, Katharine McPhee, Kellie Pickler, Mandisa, Bucky Covington, and Taylor Hicks. In fact, as the show headed into its final weeks in the spring of 2006, *Entertainment Weekly* dubbed season five "the biggest *Idol* ever." Said Simon,

“It's the only year there hasn't been a front-runner. You could argue the ones who should do well would be Kellie, Taylor, and Chris. Based on technical merit, you'd have to give it to Chris and Katharine. It's a strange year and because of that, I'm enjoying it more.”

Chorus of Boos

Chris had a scare on April 19, finishing in the bottom three in the voting after singing "What a Wonderful World" by jazz immortal Louis Armstrong. He returned the next week to give a powerful performance of the Bryan Adams love song "Have You Ever Really Loved A Woman." The following week, he rocked the house with "Renegade" by Styx.

By early May, after 13 weeks of the competition, there were four competitors still standing: Chris, Katharine, Elliott, and Taylor. By now, the buzz in the **tabloid** press and on the Internet was hottest for Chris—clearly, he had emerged as the favorite. *Entertainment Weekly* put the odds at 2 to 1 that Chris would win the competition while Katharine stood at 3 to 1, Taylor at 4 to 1, and Elliott at 10 to 1. Said the magazine, "The bald boy can tackle the perilous theme nights—from Stevie

CHRIS AND VIN: SEPARATED AT BIRTH?

When Chris started losing his hair, he shaved his whole head. No one seemed to notice back home in North Carolina, but soon after Chris started performing on national TV the celebrity magazines as well as the Internet started buzzing with talk that Chris is a dead-on look-alike for action movie actor Vin Diesel, star of such films as *The Chronicles of Riddick*, *The Fast and the Furious*, and *Babylon A.D.* People magazine even speculated that Chris earned extra votes because of his resemblance to the tough-guy film actor. Wrote *People*,

“His cred as a bona-fide rocker—plus that whole Vin Diesel thing—may give him the best shot at true idoldom.”

Chris's powerful singing style landed him among the final four contestants. His wide-ranging talent helped him become an *Idol* fan favorite, so he was shocked to be suddenly voted off. At first Chris was devastated; later he saw it as an opportunity to explore new options.

Wonder to country—and still give performances that are undeniably his. . . . Chris gives us what we are hungry for."

On May 9, Chris performed stirring covers of two Elvis Presley hits—"Suspicious Minds" and "A Little Less Conversation"—and then, on the following night, he was shocked to learn that he had been voted off the show. The news was delivered on national TV by *American Idol*'s host, Ryan Seacrest, who said, "A lot of people predicted Chris, that you could be the next 'American Idol.' . . . Chris, you are going home tonight. This journey ends."

The judges were stunned—Randy, Simon, and Paula were speechless. Paula even started sobbing. As for Chris, viewers at home could see the disappointment in his face. Later, Chris said,

> **"It was definitely a shock at that moment in time. You're in a contest and you get to a point where you want to win it. That's why you got in it."**

As Ryan made the announcement, a chorus of boos rained down in the TV studio. Chris's fans in the audience found themselves in denial. Many cried as Chris closed the broadcast giving one more performance of "Suspicious Minds." After the show, Chris said,

> **"Randy was pretty much saying, 'Don't worry about it, you're going to be fine.' Paula was crying too much to say anything. And Simon was shocked. He said he didn't see this coming and wished me the best of luck and totally believes in me. I think things are going to be O.K."**

The Bigger Picture

There is no question that Chris's ouster from *Idol* was a shocking development that was unexpected by producers of the show as

Taylor Hicks triumphed as the *Idol* season 5 winner, mainly because of his rare gifts in belting out soul and rhythm and blues numbers. After *Idol*, Taylor's first album was certified platinum, and he later went on tour in the musical *Grease*.

well as the fans at home. In fact, many *American Idol* fans later complained that when they called in their votes for Chris, the ballots were recorded in error for Katharine. Chris also believes that some of his supporters, feeling he had the competition sewed up, cast sympathy votes for Katharine, Taylor, and Elliott. Whatever the reason, Chris went home two weeks before the end of the competition, which Taylor eventually won. Said Chris,

❝I wasn't going to pretend to be happy about it. It was definitely a gut-wrenching

moment. I wasn't expecting it, not even a little bit. It was definitely a low blow for me. It didn't feel good but I try to look at the positive and see the bigger picture and say, 'You know what? Maybe this is the right thing. Maybe this is just a big opportunity for many doors to open.'

I was expecting [Deanna] to be, you know, out of control, and I would have to be the one to console her, but I think it was the other way around. She was really just telling me how proud she was of me. She was sorry it happened but she said big things happen for a reason. We have to hang on and see what that is and believe there's a bigger picture there. **"**

TAYLOR HICKS: SEASON FIVE'S WINNER

Born October 7, 1976, Taylor Hicks was 29 years old when he won on *American Idol*, making him the oldest winner ever of the competition. During the 2006 competition, Taylor made his mark performing the soul and rhythm and blues songs he learned as a teenager in suburban Birmingham, Alabama.

At the age of 16, Taylor discovered he had perfect pitch, meaning he could hear musical notes and then replicate them on the harmonica and guitar—two instruments he taught himself—as well as with his voice. "I would start playing off different sounds that I heard around my house and repeat solos that I heard on a record or the radio without practicing them," he said.

After winning on *American Idol*, Taylor recorded an album, *Taylor Hicks*, which was certified platinum in January 2007, a month after its release. Since then, though, Taylor's label has dropped him, evidently disappointed in the album's sales. In 2009 Taylor self-produced his second album, *The Distance*, and has also made TV appearances and toured in a road company of the musical *Grease*, portraying the character of the Teen Angel.

Chris's disappointment at losing *Idol* didn't last long. Soon after the show, he was bombarded with offers for record deals. He released his version of Bon Jovi's "Wanted Dead or Alive," which rocketed to the top of the charts, largely thanks to his still-loyal fan base.

4

Heading to the Top of the Charts

For Chris, the pain of losing on *American Idol* turned out to be very brief. After turning in stellar performances on the show over the course of four months, Chris had developed a devoted base of fans who could be counted on to follow his career as it moved beyond *Idol.*

Soon, Chris was flooded with offers from music producers, including 19 Entertainment, which produces *American Idol.* Executives from the company, which guarantees big record contracts for *Idol* winners, moved quickly to sign Chris. A few weeks later, 19 Entertainment announced it had inked a deal with then-RCA Records head Clive Davis to release Chris's first album.

Meanwhile, Chris's cover of the Bon Jovi hit "Wanted Dead or Alive," which he had performed on *Idol*, was released as a single.

The song quickly moved into *Billboard* magazine's Hot 100 chart. He also made the rounds of the talk shows, appearing as a guest on *The Tonight Show with Jay Leno*, *The Today Show*, *Live With Regis and Kelly*, and *The Ellen DeGeneres Show*.

No Hard Feelings

Regardless of where Chris appeared, the hosts always had the same question: Did he feel cheated by getting voted off *Idol*? Chris always answered no, and that he accepted the audience's vote. Still, the controversy never seemed to die down. When former

After *Idol*, Chris demonstrated his rocking style on the TV talk show circuit, including the *Ellen DeGeneres Show*. Several hosts fueled a continuing controversy, asking if he was still sad about the end of his *Idol* competition. But Chris was so busy dealing with the many opportunities coming his way that he quickly had gotten over his loss.

presidents George H.W. Bush and Bill Clinton appeared on *The Ellen DeGeneres Show* to raise money for the survivors of Hurricane Katrina, host Ellen DeGeneres jokingly asked them if they could also do something to help Chris Daughtry.

For Chris, the notoriety and opportunities that were now coming his way took a lot of the sting out of losing on *Idol*. He said,

> **"It took me about two days to get over it. I was like, 'You know what? Keep going with it and move on.' Next thing you know, Clive Davis wanted to meet with me, and the rest is history."**

TURNING DOWN HIS IDOLS

Soon after leaving *Idol*, Chris found himself flooded with offers. One intriguing feeler was put out by the hard rock group Fuel, which asked Chris to join the group as its new lead singer. Chris has always been a fan of Fuel. In his second week on *Idol*, Chris performed the band's hit "Hemorrhage (In My Hands)," giving the song a boost in MP3 sales as well as renewing interest in the band's 2000 album, *Something Like Human*, on which the single had appeared. A few weeks later, *Idol* judge Randy Jackson disclosed that Fuel approached Chris about joining the band at the conclusion of the *Idol* competition.

Hours after Chris's last appearance on *American Idol*, Fuel band members Jeff Abercrombie and Carl Bell appeared on the TV show *Extra* and renewed the offer to Chris. "Chris, if you are watching, we've talked about this before, and if you want to entertain it again we'll take it and go," said Abercrombie. Contacted by reporters, Chris acknowledged that he was giving the Fuel offer considerable thought. Eventually he declined, opting to develop his own music.

Away from Home

RCA lined up some of the major rock songwriters in the business to work with Chris on writing the cuts for his debut album, including Carl Bell from Fuel, Rob Thomas from Matchbox Twenty, and Mitch Allan from SR-71. In fact, Chris had a hand in writing all but two of the 12 tracks on the album. That Thanksgiving, just six months after leaving *Idol*, RCA released the album, titled *Daughtry*.

Two singles from the album, "It's Not Over" and "Home," were immediate successes. "It's Not Over," a love song told from the perspective of a man recently released from prison, peaked at number 4 on *Billboard*'s Hot 100 chart and made the list of top 40 downloads on iTunes. "Home," which tells the story of a rock star who misses his family, climbed to fifth place on *Billboard*'s Hot 100.

Chris wrote the song a day before he left his home in McLeansville to begin his run on *Idol*. Chris said he was thinking a lot about how much he was going to miss Deanna and the children while living in Hollywood. He said,

> **"I was at home, actually sitting on my couch. I knew I was going to go away and do the show and I'd never been away from my family for that long. I got into the mind-set of what that was going to be like. I picked up the guitar and wasn't planning on writing anything and started humming along and wrote the thing in, like, 10 minutes."**

Idol Theme Song

"Home" was adopted as an *Idol* theme song and is played after contestants are voted off. At the end of the sixth season, Chris made a personal appearance on *Idol* to perform the song as the last contestant was eliminated and a winner declared.

Two other singles from the album also found success on the charts. The love ballad "Feels Like Tonight" hit the top position on *Billboard*'s Adult Top 40 chart. And "What About Now," a call for people to respond to poverty, environmental concerns, and other social issues, reached eighth place on *Billboard*'s Hot Digital Songs chart and also placed within the top 20 on the *Billboard* Hot 100 chart. Chris donated royalties from the single to Idol Gives Back, the charity sponsored by the *American Idol* producers, and to help sell the song Daughtry recorded a music video on location in an impoverished village in the African nation of Uganda.

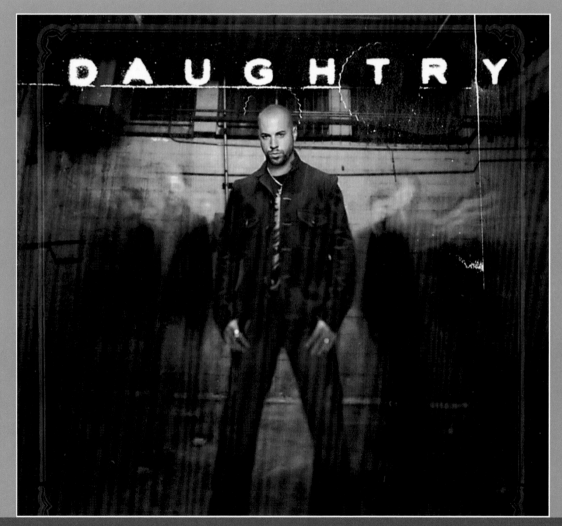

Only six months after leaving *Idol,* Chris released his first album, *Daughtry.* He was lucky to collaborate with some major rock songwriters and was proud of his own developing writing skills. Fans agreed; four of his singles jumped to the top of the charts.

Chris returned to the season 7 finale of *Idol* to sing his hit, "Home." The single had become hugely popular and told the story of a rock star who missed his family. In fact, "Home" was adopted as a theme song by *American Idol* and played when contestants were voted off.

Mixed Reviews

Despite wide anticipation for the album in the music community, the reviews for *Daughtry* were mixed. Critics praised Chris's talent but suggested he played it too safe on the album, sticking too closely to his hard rock roots and not making a true effort to expand his range. "If front-running rocker Chris Daughtry's dismissal from *American Idol* shocked millions last season, his debut album should surprise no one," huffed the rock critic for *Billboard*. "This music is tailor-made for . . . consumers whose taste has already been well-established."

People magazine's music critic, Chuck Arnold, called *Daughtry* "a solid if not spectacular effort" while Christian Hoard of *Rolling Stone* wrote, "The debut album from former *American Idol* semifinalist Chris Daughtry makes one thing clear: Homeboy loves to rock."

The music critics may have been lukewarm to *Daughtry*, but Chris's fans knew what they liked. The album quickly went platinum and gained four nominations for Grammy Awards. It remained on the *Billboard* Top 200 album chart for an impressive 104 weeks. At the end of 2007, *Billboard* declared *Daughtry* the top-selling album of 2007, beating out *The Duchess* by pop singer Fergie and *Konvicted* by **hip-hop** star Akon. "The final numbers are in," wrote *Billboard*,

> **". . . and the *Billboard* album sales champion for 2007 is *Daughtry*. . . . The former *American Idol* loser was a big winner on the charts."**

Overall, Chris couldn't have been more satisfied with his initial effort. He said,

> **"I never expected [success] to happen this early in my career. I always hoped I would be playing a bar and a record guy would hear me and want to do something."**

Busy Tour Schedule

Chris had to work hard to sell the album, meaning he had to go on tour. To accompany Chris, RCA helped him organize a touring band, which was named Daughtry. Initial members of the band included guitarists Jeremy Brady and Josh Steely, bassist Josh Paul, and drummer Joey Barnes. Like Chris, Brady and Barnes were from North Carolina and Chris had known them since before auditioning for *Idol*. Brady has since left the band, though, and has been replaced by guitarist Brian Craddock.

Starting in January 2007, Daughtry went on an international tour. The band played concerts across America and Canada and also performed in Great Britain, Germany, Australia, and Singapore. In some of those concerts, Daughtry performed as the opening act for Bon Jovi, but for several dates Chris's band was the headliner.

In May, Daughtry appeared at the pre-race concert staged at the Indianapolis 500. A few weeks later, Chris and the band were the headline act at Summerfest in Milwaukee, Wisconsin, where they performed before an audience of some 15,000 fans. And in September, Daughtry performed at the pre-race concert for the Chevy Rock & Roll 400, a NASCAR race in Richmond, Virginia. In all, Chris performed before 265 audiences in 2007.

It was a hectic, exhausting schedule, but Chris and Daughtry kept the energy level high and always delivered for their audiences. Chris said he was not surprised by the warm reception Daughtry received from fans during the tour. He said,

❝People relate to [our music] because it's pretty simple, everyday stuff. We all come from a blue-collar background, and I think the majority of America connects with that. We've worked our butts off all our life to get where we are. And people see that. We're not just some band that got lucky. We've definitely put in our time in the clubs, playing for the workers or maybe 15 people at the most. It's definitely paid off.❞

Moving Beyond *Idol*

As Chris and the members of Daughtry kept up a busy tour schedule, the other competitors from *Idol*'s fifth season were also finding success in the music industry.

Elliott lasted a week longer than Chris but was also voted off the show, while Katharine made it to the finals, finishing second to Taylor. Clearly, Katharine and Elliott were both talented singers

To support his album, Chris went on tour with his new band, Daughtry. It was a hectic, exhausting experience, but the group worked hard to keep their energy high. Fans everywhere responded to their powerful style, and enthusiastic crowds swelled every concert venue.

and both were offered recording deals at the conclusion of the show. Katharine, a tall rhythm and blues singer with traffic-stopping beauty, released the album *Katharine McPhee* in January 2007. The album could muster only modest sales, though. Still, Katharine has won some roles in TV and films and appears to be pursuing an acting career, indicating that she may have a bright future before the cameras.

Since leaving *Idol*, Elliott has released two albums, titled *Elliott Yamin* and *Fight for Love*. Both albums have recorded strong sales

In addition to appearing in North America, the 2007 Daughtry tour took Chris to Australia, Great Britain, Germany, and Singapore. They played more than 250 appearances worldwide. Sometimes the band opened for Chris's idol, Bon Jovi, but often they rocked the crowd as headliners.

and Elliott continues to record and tour. Other contestants from the fifth season include Kellie, Mandisa, and Bucky. All have moved beyond *American Idol* and recorded albums, and all have won success in the recording industry.

CLAY AIKEN: LOOKS CAN DECEIVE

In the second season of *American Idol*, top contestants Ruben Studdard and Clay Aiken battled down to the wire, with Ruben emerging as the winner. Despite losing in the final vote, Clay has gone on to compile a vibrant career as a singer, releasing five albums since 2003. He has also acted on TV and appeared on Broadway in the role of Sir Robin in the musical *Spamalot*, a spoof of the King Arthur legend.

When he auditioned in early 2003, Clay hardly seemed as though he was on the road to stardom. Nevertheless he let go with a strong rendition of the love song "Always and Forever." The performance shocked Simon and Randy. "You don't look like a pop star but you've got a great voice," said Simon. Added Randy, "It's just really wild for me to hear this voice come out of this 'look,' but he can sing."

But no competitor from the fifth season—not even the eventual winner, Taylor—has matched Chris in album sales, concert dates, or Grammy nominations. As a very busy 2007 came to an end, Chris knew that his career had moved well beyond *American Idol.* He said,

❝On [*American Idol*], I wasn't able to do fully what I'm capable of; that was just, to me, a way of showing my voice off. This is a totally different thing. This is who we are— we're musicians, we write our own music, and it's a totally different ballgame.❞

In 2008, Chris performed to help raise money for worthy charities, tried acting, won three American Music Awards, and hung out with several of his heroes from the rock and roll world. But Chris doesn't let his popularity go to his head and always stays true to his hard-rocking roots.

5

True to His Hard-Rocking Roots

For Chris, 2008 got off to a controversial start when, in an interview with *Rolling Stone*, he criticized *American Idol*, suggesting that the show is growing stale and suffering from a lack of talent. During the interview, Chris said he finds it hard to watch the show and suggested *Idol* is in danger of losing its audience.

He also criticized the producers for concentrating too much on the untalented wannabes whose pathetic but very humorous auditions kick off the start of each season. "We've already seen all the people who can't sing," Chris complained. "It's the same thing every year. They should be finding people who are artists and trying to develop that."

He also called on the producers to let contestants perform songs they have written themselves and also accompany themselves on guitars, pianos, or other instruments. That type of competition, Chris said, would truly reveal the most talented performers. He told the *Rolling Stone* reporter,

Chris caused a controversy when he criticized *American Idol,* saying the show's format was getting old and that the judges focused too much on the funny but untalented contestants. He later apologized, but the show's ratings had actually fallen, and many music insiders agreed with his comments.

"Why don't you give them a time to perform some of their own songs if they're able to play an instrument? Let's see what kind of artists they really are . . . People would end up taking it more seriously."

Public Apology

Many music insiders agreed with Chris's remarks, pointing out that some winners on *Idol*, particularly Taylor and Ruben Studdard from season two, had failed to rack up strong album sales and had, in fact, been dropped by their labels—an indication that, perhaps, they had not been the strongest contestants in the seasons in which they competed. Moreover, while season five had been regarded as one of the best *Idol* seasons ever, season six had been something of a disappointment. That year, **ratings** for the show dropped for the first time since its debut in 2002.

WHAT IS CHRIS DAUGHTRY–ITIS?

Simon Cowell has found reason to agree with Chris's criticisms of the show. Simon says many of the performers suffer from "Chris Daughtry–itis" and "Jennifer Hudson–itis," which he described as a belief that they don't have to win to make it big in the recording industry. Jennifer is the *Idol* competitor who, after being voted off the show, went on to win an Academy Award for her role in the film *Dreamgirls* and record a hit album.

Simon believes that attitude hurts the show as well as the performers, because they stop listening to what the judges have to say, knowing they are virtually guaranteed a recording contract simply for making it into the top 10. He says, "I think we suffer from Jennifer Hudson– and Chris Daughtry–itis, which is people who didn't win get great careers and now a lot of contestants believing it absolutely doesn't matter."

Still, executives at *Idol* and others connected with the show felt stung by Chris's remarks. Randy told a reporter,

> **“I love Chris. I think he made an amazing record that he sold extremely well. He's a testament to the fact that no matter where you finish on _Idol_—even if you finish 12th—if you make a great record and you got that kind of exposure, the public will resoundingly buy it. But the bottom line is there would be no Chris Daughtry if there wasn't _American Idol_.”**

A few days after Chris's words were published, he made a public apology and retracted his criticisms. He said,

> **“My long-winded point is this: I was never trying to 'diss' the show or bite the hand that fed me, so to speak. I was simply giving my input on what I think would spice the show up a bit. Sorry for being honest.”**

In early 2008, as the seventh season of _Idol_ got underway, it became evident that the show's producers had come to some of the same conclusions as Chris, and shortly before the season's kickoff they made some adjustments to the show in an effort to create more electricity. For example, they spent more time airing stories about the competitors' backgrounds. The producers also announced they would permit the contestants in the early rounds to play instruments while performing.

Mingling With Celebrities

Soon after the controversy died down, Chris attended the Grammy Awards in Los Angeles. He was not asked to perform during the nationally televised awards show, which many insiders believed was a slight. On the other hand, Clive Davis, the powerful music executive who signed Chris to his record deal, invited him to perform at his pre-Grammy party, which is regarded as

The 2008 season winner David Cook performs on *American Idol* playing his guitar. The producers had changed the rules to keep the excitement level high; they now allowed contestants in the early rounds to play instruments.

one of the most coveted invitations in the music industry. Chris performed two songs during the event.

While performing at the party, Chris met British singing star Leona Lewis as well as Slash, the veteran guitarist from the hard rocking group Guns N' Roses. Chris admitted to being a bit star struck while mingling with the celebrities he met at Davis's party. "Just to be associated with an elite group of people who have been in the business so long is an awesome thing," he said.

Although he would fall short in the competition for the 2008 Grammy Awards, a few months earlier Chris won three trophies at

Chris and his band members clown with their 2008 American Music Award for Favorite Pop-Rock, Band, Duo, or Group. That year they kept up their busy touring schedule, and their loyal fans followed them to events across the country.

the American Music Awards for Best Pop-Rock Album, Best Adult Contemporary Artist, and Best New Artist. He also performed during the nationally televised awards show. A year later, Chris and the other members of Daughtry returned to the American Music Awards to accept the award for Favorite Pop-Rock, Band, Duo, or Group.

Trying Hand on Acting

Meanwhile, Chris and his band kept up a busy schedule, performing at a number of major events including a pre-game concert at the first Arizona Cardinals home game of the year. He also made a non-singing appearance before the cameras, acting in an episode of the TV crime drama *CSI: NY*.

The plot for the episode concerned the hunt for a deranged serial killer who targets people named "Mac Taylor," which is the name of the detective on the show played by star Gary Sinise. Chris played a character named "Machiavelli Taylor," described in the show's **script** as "an attractive 30-something-year-old musician."

Other celebrities also appearing on the show and playing characters named Mac Taylor included actress Rumer Willis and actor Scott Wolf. Chris's time on camera was brief, but he shared a scene with Sinise, a veteran actor, in which his character expressed frustration at being summoned to a police precinct house and told his life is in danger.

IDOL'S MOST FAMOUS FLOPS

Not all *American Idol* contestants go on to successful recording careers. Some singers whose performances on *Idol* truly captured the attention of fans have, nevertheless, fallen off the radar screen soon after the end of the season.

In *Idol*'s first season, Kelly Clarkson and Justin Guarini staged a riveting battle with Kelly edging Justin in the finals. Soon after the season ended, Kelly and Justin starred in a critically panned film, *From Justin to Kelly*. Kelly then went on to release several top-selling albums. Justin also released an album, titled *Justin Guarini*, but it posted dismal sales of just 143,000 copies.

Another *Idol* competitor struggling to achieve stardom is Tamyra Gray, who also competed on the first season. During the competition, Paula compared Tamyra to Whitney Houston, Céline Dion, and Mariah Carey, but her album chalked up modest sales.

Among the other notable flops are Paris Bennett, a season five contender whose album sold just some 21,000 copies; Blake Lewis, the runner-up in season six whose album registered a disappointing 286,000 in sales, and Constantine Maroulis, a season four contender whose album managed to post just 23,000 in sales.

Doing Good

Chris also found time to perform in charitable events. In 2008 he returned to *The Ellen DeGeneres Show* where he performed "Home" accompanied by the African Children's Choir, which he took on tour to help raise money for the ONE Campaign. The ONE Campaign was co-founded by singer Bono of the rock group U2 to raise money to fight poverty and eradicate the deadly disease AIDS in Africa. Said Chris,

> **When things started going well. . . I said, 'We have to do something to start giving back. The ONE Campaign was interested in talking to me and I was interested in them as well. . . . It seemed like a beautiful thing to be a part of.**

As part of his work for the ONE Campaign, Chris performed at the 2008 Democratic National Convention in Denver, Colorado, as well as that year's Republican National Convention in Minneapolis, Minnesota, to help raise the profile of the charity among the nation's most powerful political leaders.

He has also done some other charitable work performing free concerts. On one occasion, he visited Children's Hospital of New York-Presbyterian and, with his band, performed two songs for a roomful of children in wheelchairs. Reporter Michael Endelman from *Entertainment Weekly* accompanied Chris to the hospital that day and wrote,

> **It's a heartbreaking scene: Frail kids in wheelchairs and teenagers tethered to IVs eagerly await this glimmer of celebrity in a sunny two-story atrium. . . .**
>
> **Daughtry gathers himself. He takes a deep breath, bounds up on stage, and performs two songs that delight the room.**

Chris feels strongly about using his fame to do good in the world. He supports his favorite charity, The ONE Campaign, by performing to raise money to fight poverty in Africa. He has toured with the African Children's Choir and has generously given free concerts for hospitals and other worthy groups.

Willing to Make Sacrifice

Keeping up such a busy schedule has made it difficult for Chris to spend much time with his young family.

For Chris, it has been a case of life imitating art since his hit song "Home" tells the story of a touring rock star who misses his family. Despite the grueling touring schedule, Chris seems, for now, willing to make the sacrifice. He said,

> **"It's tough . . . There's so much I don't know about my kids when I get home. [I say], 'Oh,**

Chris is always keenly aware that his fans helped him on his journey from struggling musician to the superstar he is today. He seems to have unlimited momentum and a memorable style that will keep his fans rocking and rolling far into the future.

I didn't know you were that tall!' So you want to take advantage of the times you are home. I don't want to look back and think that I missed opportunities to make memories with my kids. "

Playing Music for His Fans

Chris has come a long way in a very short time. He has gone from being an unknown hard rock singer, bouncing from small-time gig to small-time gig, into an international superstar whose future seems unlimited. Sometime in 2009, Chris and his band expect to release a second album. Chris has been careful not to talk too much about the album before its release, but he promises that it will remain true to his hard-rocking roots—the type of music he knows his fans will appreciate. Of his fans, Chris says,

"The . . . intensity, the way they sing along at our shows, the radio and video support— I don't think the average person understands how crucial it is for a band to know you've got that net underneath you. To start out as a fan with a dream, and then to go from a struggling musician with the same hopes and aspirations as so many others and to be able to fulfill some of those dreams, well, I feel like we're all part of this incredible movement. I'm so aware of what it took to get here. I can't help but appreciate what an honor it is to keep it rolling. "

1979 Chris Daughtry born in Roanoke Rapids, North Carolina, on December 26.

1996 Learns to play the guitar.

1998 Graduates from Fluvanna High School in Palmyra, Virginia.

2000 Marries Deanna Robertson.

2002 *American Idol* premiers on the Fox network.

2005 Forms the band Absent Element.

Auditions for the CBS reality show *Rock Star: INXS*.

2006 Places fourth on *American Idol*.

Turns down an offer from Fuel to join the band as lead singer.

Releases first album, *Daughtry*, which is certified platinum.

2007 With his new band, Daughtry, begins international tour.

Chris and the album *Daughtry* nominated for four Grammy Awards.

Chris and his band, Daughtry, win three American Music Awards.

2008 Performs at the gala pre-Grammy party hosted by music executive Clive Davis.

Appears in a non-singing role in an episode of *CSI: NY*.

In comments to *Rolling Stone*, criticizes *American Idol*, saying the show has grown stale.

2009 Releases second album.

2006 Places fourth on *American Idol*.

2007 *Daughtry* receives American Music Awards for Best Pop-Rock Album; Chris is awarded Best Adult Contemporary Artist and Best New Artist.

Daughtry certified platinum; eventually, the album will sell more than four million copies.

Sings the National Anthem at the National Football Conference title game in Chicago.

"Home" selected as a theme song for *American Idol*, played as contestants are voted off the show.

Billboard magazine declares *Daughtry* the top selling album of the year.

2008 Performs at the Democratic and Republican national conventions to help raise money for the ONE Campaign, an African relief group.

Chris and his band Daughtry win the American Music Award for Favorite Pop-Rock, Band, Duo, or Group.

Daughtry nominated for a Grammy Award for Best Rock Album; "It's Not Over" nominated for Grammys for Best Rock Performance by a Duo or Group and Best Rock Song, and "Home" nominated for Best Pop Performance by a Duo or Group with Vocals.

"Home" awarded People's Choice Award for Favorite Rock Song.

country and western—Modern style of music that traces its roots to the folk songs performed by singers and musicians in the southern and Appalachian portions of America.

genres—Categories of pieces of music that share a certain style or theme.

gigs—Opportunities for musicians to earn money for performing.

hip-hop—Style of music that usually dispenses with the melody in favor of a rhymed patter known as raps.

jazz—Style of music with roots in the African-American community, often featuring an improvisational sound and reliance on the piano and saxophone to provide the melodies and bass fiddle to keep the beat.

martial arts—Hand-to-hand combat, developed mostly in Asian nations, that includes such forms of fighting as karate and jujitsu.

platinum—In the music industry, a distinction awarded to an album that has sold at least a million copies.

pop—Short for popular music, pop songs usually feature strong melodies and a heavy reliance on vocals; the songs are typically produced so they can be played in less than four minutes to accommodate radio station formats.

ratings—Sizes of the audiences that tune in to particular television or radio programs.

rhythm and blues—Style of dance music with roots in the African-American community, often reflecting an urban influence and enormously influential on other genres, including rock.

rock—Style of music that has dominated American entertainment since the 1950s; played mostly with electrically amplified instruments maintaining a loud, fast, and pulsating beat.

script—Written directions to actors and others involved in productions of plays and films, giving them stage directions as well as the dialogue to be spoken in the scenes.

tabloid—Style of journalism practiced in newspapers, TV, and the Internet that focuses on celebrity news and gossip and bizarre crimes; popularized during the 1920s by newspapers published in tabloid format, meaning they were half the size of standard newspapers.

Books

Giddens, Sandra. *Chris Daughtry*. New York: Rosen Center, 2008.

Jackson, Laura. *Jon Bon Jovi*. New York: Citadel, 2005.

Tracy, Kathleen. *Chris Daughtry*. Hockessin, DE: Mitchell Lane, 2007.

Periodicals

Endelman, Michael. "The Anti-Idol." *Entertainment Weekly* no. 922 (February 23, 2007): p. 72.

Graff, Gary. "Chris Daughtry." *Billboard* vol. 119, no. 51 (December 22, 2007): p. 54.

Gunderson, Edna. "It's Just the Beginning for Chris Daughtry; *Idol* Also-Ran Rocks the Charts His Way." *USA Today* (March 21, 2007): p. D-1.

Scaggs, Austin. "Chris Daughtry." *Rolling Stone* no. 1,023 (April 5, 2007): p. 30.

Shaw, Jessica. "The Biggest Idol Ever." *Entertainment Weekly* no. 873 (April 21, 2006): p. 34.

Web Sites

http://abc.go.com/primetime/ama/index?pn=index

Maintained by the ABC television network, the Web site for the American Music Awards lists the current winners, provides photos and biographies of the winners and performers, and provides access for fans to blog about the show.

www.americanidol.com

By accessing *American Idol*'s official Web site, fans can read biographies of the competitors, view photos and videos, and read the latest news about the show and the performers. By accessing the site's Alumni News link, fans can find updates for many of the performers in *American Idol*'s past seasons.

www.daughtryofficial.com

At Chris's official Web site, visitors can read a biography of Chris, add comments to a blog, view videos of Chris and his band, check the band's touring schedule, and read news updates on the band's activities.

www.grammy.com

At the official Web site of the Grammy Awards, visitors can find a list of current winners and view photos and videos of the annual awards show. By using the site's search engine, visitors can search for Grammy winners back to 1958.

page

ABOUT THE AUTHOR

Hal Marcovitz is a former newspaper reporter who has written more than 100 books for young readers. In 2005, *Nancy Pelosi*, his biography of House Speaker Nancy Pelosi, was named to *Booklist* magazine's list of recommended feminist books for young readers. He lives in Chalfont, Pennsylvania, with his wife Gail and daughter Ashley.